Black **Rose**

Marah H

Contents

My Black **Rose**;

You are something beautiful in a way that is least expected

From every petal and every thorn

And although the world may never appreciate your magic

/I will accept that/

It is enough to be appreciated all alone

You are a complex mess

Still learning who you're becoming

From the way you love and how you'll grow

Till the end and from the very beginning

I will always hold you close

In every corner of my very soul

Learning to embrace you, I slowly will

The part of me you have always been

Allowing you to seep into my heart

And accepting that you have always been a part of my skin

I: Roots

I had these reassuring thoughts
that everything will be easy
but because no one voices their difficulties
it's like I'm the only one with these feelings
/I have never felt so lonely/

You ask me what's wrong
and I want to stay silent
but I say it's nothing
because I don't want you to see the
damage built up inside me
& maybe it's better off that way -
for me to feel it alone
and deal with it all on my own.

<u>As if</u>

You always tell me I'm beautiful
You always tell me you love me
As if you want to reassure me
As if you know I doubt myself

Sometimes I wish I could cry
But I'm always on the verge of it
And it's like a storm is constantly stirring inside of me
Threatening to do more and more damage
Every time I hold it in

I need more than reassurance
Especially when it gets like this
This hard,
My body is holding in all of this pain
that I am desperate to release
& I am stuck with it
I need someone to remove it from me
I need someone to hold my hand
and take me away from my worries

I hope I don't give up on what makes me happy
because of my self-destructive sense of worthlessness

I'm not sure where i fit in
I feel like i've changed myself so much
Trying to squeeze into all of the tight spaces
To make others' lives easier
That sometimes i wonder
If i'm needed here at all
/i've shrunken myself so much, even i have forgotten my
own existence/

You don't see pain
Even when it's staring you in the face
Crying for your attention

The fragility of life

I think I had only begun to understand what it meant to be alive when I learnt that it could take anything for someone to not want to know it anymore

<u>you never really can fix a heart</u>

I was sad
And I didn't know why
All I knew was I had to deal with it somehow
Not to be happy
But to feel it a little less

Thanatos

I didn't know it would hurt as much as it did,
but I know that I let the pain grow more and more
when I could have stopped it.

I just want someone to tell me that in spite of everything,
it will be okay

For my own sanity, I keep looking for people with the right
words to say to me
to keep me together for even a moment longer

It's funny
I don't feel the pain I cause myself
until I see the scars.

Envy

I lost all of my self-confidence
thinking that I was the only person that existed like me
and you were the only person that existed like you.

I can't live
because I only ever wonder when things will turn bad for me
every time I feel happy.

Conversations with myself

You told me you'd help me
every time I fell apart
but instead, you let me crumble
at my own feet.
you told me you'd protect me from the pain I felt
by hiding it
but it's the only thing I can see.

Maybe it drives you crazy
to feel so much
even though you pretend not to feel at all

You don't feel the weight
that I do
you get to walk freely
reaching for whatever makes you happy
whilst I can barely lift a finger

My worries are like a string that I must travel along with no sign of
an end
and no balance to keep me from falling into the abyss

Cloudy skies

I sometimes forget
that there's a world outside of my head
I've become so accustomed to living here
that the grey and blues that I see in the sky
aren't so different to the ones in my mind

My insecurities dig at me like a knife
I don't know how to move away or where to go
although I keep avoiding every mirror to make it disappear
I see the shards,
broken pieces of my reflection on the floor

<u>Reckless</u>

I go about this place
/my mind/
restlessly causing myself pain
as if I find joy in it

I have become so accustomed to the dark
that I'd look for black holes
in a cluster of stars

<u>Ellipsis…</u>

Time keeps passing by me
and here I am
infinitely stuck in this moment
wondering how I fit into all of this

<u>Wilting flower</u>

Sometimes I feel like
a flower that is wilting instead of blooming
regardless of how much sunlight and rain I am given

I'm afraid that
because I dream of things so much
bigger than me
I will live a life where I'm constantly
wishing for something more

Truthfully,
I have always felt like an afterthought
like sparks above a kindling flame
I could scream and echoes of a whisper
would fill a room
almost like unneeded space

I grew in your shadow
& that's why
I'm so unknown to myself
I let you dim my light
and I never learnt to
flourish

I have exhausted all of my words
till my pen ran dry and my thoughts became
empty
how much more must I write of pain
before it leaves me

Responsibility

Sometimes I'm unsure if you love me
sometimes I wonder if I'm the burden
that stops you from sleeping at night

How much presence do I truly have in this world;
could I leave and would the ground I stand on collapse without me?
will anyone think of me when they see something beautiful,
or when they look up and see the stars?
I wonder if the roses I so persistently wished to blossom would
finally do so
& stay
would something here remain alive on my behalf?
because sometimes I wonder
if I do too little to make the world love me

Highs & Lows

Pink fingers reach for the warmth of the sun
but the coldness pressing on her soul
weighs her down to the soil

For it is in these lows
that she is made to envy the skies
accompanies by thorns

And in her highs,
she must make her bed among wildflowers
to relieve her from her sorrows

Black **Rose**   Marah H

you're right
i can be cold sometimes
i act like nothing affects me
but i feel sorrow so often
that i've had to learn
to not let the flames engulf me

Sometimes I want someone to hurt me more
So this pain would hurt less

And you see her like she's everything
And I'm nothing
And I've even begun to feel like that

I'm okay until I'm not

And you often tell me
that I'm strong enough
and I feel good when I hear it
until it stops
and I'm back to square one

Growing problems in the place of solutions

I might pour myself out one day
and empty myself of these emotions
but I'm afraid that when that happens
I'll create weeds instead of flowers

It feels like
every opportunity that lies ahead
is inaccessible to me,
I guess I'm so afraid
that my touch is so harmful
that it may set any good thing ablaze
I wish I spread blossoming flowers
from my palms
instead of reckless flames

I look at you and try to find pieces of me in your eyes
but all I see is my reflection
and a sorrowful attempt
to try and be someone different

Maybe sometimes
I am not enough
but this is all I have
& all I have is what you see
and I can't make myself any different for you
I can't even make myself any different for me
so maybe
instead of making me feel less than anyone else
maybe you should just let me breathe
stop suffocating me with your demeaning behaviour
for once, I wish you'd just let me be

I clench my fists to keep hold of all of these happy moments for
longer
but the feeling doesn't last and they seem to slip between my fingers
I wish I knew how people deal with these instances
because for me
it's like trying to hold water

You make my worries your own
and it makes me wish you didn't love me so much
because I don't want you to suffer from something
that I'm not sure will ever end.

I can't help the way I am
and I don't want to make you like this too
but you love me so much
that you want to understand why I feel the way that I do
and I know,
if we carry on like this
you're going to wither away
and I can't have that
I can't have you tearing yourself apart
trying to 'fix' me
because I know I can't fix you

I didn't want to be the one
to teach you how to hurt

but I didn't learn how to love
without needing to let go
/I'm not strong enough to love the way you do/

Overthinking

I don't know how to push these thoughts aside
I've never learnt how to build that barrier
it controls me
and all I ask is that you listen
so it doesn't
completely take over me

II: Plucked

Black **Rose**

Marah H

this heart has beared scratches its entire life
but you pierced it completely;
why can it not bear a stronger pain
if it has persisted through so many?

Black **Rose** Marah H

i wish i could go back
& break your heart instead

I don't love you
I love how you can make me forget
But when that moment ends
The pain is terrible
I hope we never speak again

i am made to observe
love existing
with me on the sidelines
/
yet
i almost had you
and i almost thought
i had someone made for me
too

I'm sorry
but i can't bear to watch
your love grow
in a place where mine
has withered

I love you

you see, it feels so strange
as if it isn't meant to be spoken out loud
~ that's how deeply i've buried these feelings now

I have
unexpectedly fallen into a pattern
of loving to a fault
& not knowing when I need to
let
go

Your garden

You don't have to worry about me
I will make myself so small
you won't notice my existence
& you can let your love flourish around me
as you want
I only ask that if I must live in your garden
please don't ever let me wilt so close to the soil
that I can never reach the sun

I have never felt wrong in the way that I have loved but I
wonder,
if my heart has broken so persistently
that it is me with this destructive nature

<u>Façade of love</u>

He opened the scars I had healed alone
and filled them with his love
as if to prove to me that it exists in him
but here I am again
having to heal wounds
that he caused
/it is moments like this that make me question what love is/

"just not yet"

And I can't shake off this voice in my head
telling me that the timing wasn't right but it will be
one day
so what do I do in the meantime,
wait forever because maybe, just maybe
you'll love me anyway?

Please don't try to push me out of your mind
if I must exist in any way
or any place
on this earth
I want to exist for you

Be careful what you say to me
because in this temporary high
where you suddenly feel like you love me
I might just believe that you genuinely do

I poured my heart into you
and created monsoons
that drowned me

And although they may love me
just as much as I deserve
I will never learn to let go of
the love I cannot have

The way I love

The way I love is unhealthy
I give more than you'd expect from me
and I don't know anyway else to show you
that I'm yours completely
without dismantling my heart
so you could hold it more comfortably

I think I hide my love for you far too well
that sometimes I'm not sure if it's filling up
every inch of me
with its burden or if it's finally slipping away

You were my sun
in all of my shadows
the light I've always craved
and in your absence
I am lost in darkness
how long must I wait for you
to lead me into your light again?

All at once
in those brief moments
you showed me what it felt like to be loved
and then
deprived me of the same love
that I barely got to taste

But my heart says there's hope
although it's silently breaking
I want to let you go
and I hate how long it's taking

<u>Take it away</u>

I have so much of my love for you in me
that I can't give
and can neither hold the weight of

You've created a stranger out of me
and now I'm having to learn who I am
all over again

Shadow

I let my soul yearn for
a love it couldn't keep
& now
I can see your shadow
where my heart used to be

And I've always dreamt you'd love my flaws
but I wish I could love them instead

Cœur de pierre

You think that
love is easy
but when you see me drown
countless times
trying to prove my love to you
you'll realise
how suffocating it can really be

You'll look for pieces of me in other people
because you know that you'll never have
all of me again

You won't understand my love
and you aren't the one to blame
I blame myself for letting it exist
if it was only going to be me feeling like this

Forever grieving

They say pain is immeasurable
but I count it by the days I don't get to see your face
the moments I don't get to hear your voice
and the instances I don't get to feel your touch

Maybe it's funny to you
to know you can manipulate someone so much
to feel in control
and to never have to learn what it could mean
to not have the power to let go

Maybe at some point earlier on, it would have been easier to tell you how I felt because of how trivial these feelings seemed.
But I wish I had known how afraid I would later become, having to hide something that has outgrown me, and now I have so much more to lose.

You left burns with every touch
and scars that only I could see
and no one understood that if I held on any longer
I wouldn't have had anything left of me

I still let myself be near you
even though I know your heart may hurt me
but I can't help but crave the feeling of safety in your arms
something that can provide me with solitude away from this
affliction
/even cages can provide some form of comfort/

I'm still not sure if it's true
But I think I lost a bit of myself
The day that I lost you

I lost touch with what was real
Who I am
When I began living in my thoughts of you

You could've told me simply that you did not understand
the pain that I was suffering
instead of pretending to know and acting like it was
nothing
& becoming a reason for me to hurt more

Looking back, I thought it was love
But I know now that it couldn't have been
Because if it was, surely it would have lasted longer and felt better
than it did

I don't know the person you have created in my mind
I am afraid of her
for she holds all of your love freely
and carelessly
without any fear or doubt of losing you
whilst I only hold your memory
/you exist more for her than you ever have for me/

I think I love people in ways
that parts of them perish with me
it explains why when I hold love in my hands for too long
they blister & ache
/I think love burns me/

You pushed your heart into my chest so forcefully,
I could no longer breathe on my own accord

III: Garden

Her eyes speak the words
that her mouth cannot form

His eyes speak the words
that his mouth cannot form

I'm afraid you'll leave
and your love will go just as quick
and I will be left wondering
/once again/
if I could ever be loved
the same

Her beauty is so ethereal
that the human eye cannot capture it completely
and still it is left in awe

<u>Every moment</u>

I hope that you never feel any less of the love that you so
selflessly give
but if that's ever the case
I promise I will provide it for you as if you've
received it a thousand times, in one moment
/maybe that would be enough/

Roses;

You're the happiness i would have
given myself
If i didn't know pain

You owe me
for making me believe that I couldn't be loved
just because I wasn't enough
for you

Unforgettable

You've always had the kind of smile that could make someone
forget how to breathe
that they exist
so how can you ever expect me to forget you?

<u>Falling in love</u>

And here it comes again
that dreaded feeling I thought I had escaped
but it just reappears in different forms
on a different face

I'll stay consistent
I'll tell you how I feel every day
I'll tell you that I love you
so there'll never be a moment that you doubt yourself
because I know how much it could hurt to not know and to never
understand.

My happiest moments were those I had spent with you but
I accept that it's time to let you go and say that this is it,
because I don't want to taint these memories and let them
make me feel something that they never did

<u>my destiny</u>

In your every walk
I hope you find your way back to me

Don't measure your love for me
by how much of her you see in me
I'd rather you not love me at all
if you cannot love me
unconditionally

You are
And maybe you will always be
A hidden reminder for me
That I can't live without *a little chaos*

i'm not ready to do more
than promise you my love
but rest assured it will come
when i know you'll give me yours

<u>no choices</u>

you took me apart
and rebuilt yourself with me
who could i ever be
but yours

He was like art
The more you look at him,
the more you fall in love with him

There's something tragic about how well the
brightest individuals can hide their sorrows

<u>Your admirer</u>

I watched your world fall apart in an instance
And surrounding you were the remnants of your heart
But you stood in the midst of it all and smiled
And for the first time, I saw a kind of strength I never
knew existed

sometimes it feels as though my life is not my own
as if i exist to see your happiness
& torment & i wonder
why i must struggle so much from the likes of you
And why you must thrive off of my misery

I begun to understand the person you were,
Someone who can hide pain so well as if it wasn't there in
the first place
Regardless of how unendurable it may be

Don't scatter your heart on the floor
And expect someone to pick up the shards
And piece them together
When there's a possibility that they'd cut themselves along the way
That's not love

All I care about
All that matters to me
Is you
And I want to know if you feel the same
Or if I'm wasting my time
giving my love away

You were the cause of your own pain
but you blamed it on everyone else
and even though you knew it yourself
you didn't want to accept it
so you'd carry around a burden
that you knew was self-inflicted

I wish you could see what I see when I look at you
maybe you'd love yourself more.

I gave all of my trust to you
And I felt my heart rip every time you held yourself back from me
I think I was afraid you'd let go without reason.

I held onto you for a while until I thought I didn't care if I let go
But honestly, I was afraid to be vulnerable in your presence
Which made me realise that I became someone around you that I
didn't want to be

And so, I carried on with my life
And left my secrets as a burden for you to keep

From all of the signs you had shown me
I couldn't see past the smile that never escaped your lips
and now I can't help but think that it was me
who let you hurt like this

I talk to you
and I realise we share the same demons in our mind
yours tell you to hold on to your sadness
and mine tell me that they're all I have

I don't know what to say to you
but I hope my presence alone
would suffice to make you feel like
you don't have to go through this on your own
because I know that I don't have much to give to help you
cope
and my words aren't enough to give you a reason to not let
go
so instead
I'll stay by you, I'll pay attention to how you feel
I'll listen
because I know you'd do that for me too
if I was in your position

it was a risk to fall in love with her
because she could make someone forget
how to love anyone else

My _poetic muse;_

you're the complex lover
that I try to fathom into words
because I don't know how to hold you any way else

I have all of the love in the world to give
but no one to give it to

/i am always giving myself flowers/

But aren't you so beautiful; and is it me who has
made you so?

I will let you live in the happiness
that I can give
but you should know
that I will take it away eventually
when I have found myself broken enough to decorate you
in contentment
that I'm sure you won't seek me again to take more

You don't need me to tell you
that there are enough reasons in this world
for you to be loved

without hesitation

She's the sun and the stars
giving me all of her light as if I deserve it
and if I ask her for the love I think I need
she'd surround every inch of my miserable sky
with all she has in a heartbeat

'The one'

I'm sure, it was too long ago for you to remember
but my love is still there, it has survived time, trials
& hatred I tried to build in my heart and mind
/towards you/
perhaps you have always been "the one" for me
& maybe our lives were too different to intertwine
that I couldn't be "the one" for you

And it is the way she smiles
that makes me realise how the sky holds the stars every
night
and leaves people in awe as if they were seeing them for
the first time

If I wanted to
I could make you live in such misery
that you wouldn't know a life without it
but we're not the same
I'm not like you
I wouldn't make you suffer from a pain
that isn't meant to be yours

How much love would it take for you
to grow flowers in the places you build your walls?

Butterfly cave

Sometimes we just want to be loved
more than we are able to love ourselves

I collect flowers from places that remind me of you
it's some form of comfort
to know that you left something beautiful in every place
you touched
and maybe I was that something beautiful too

But you keep crashing into me like waves of an ocean
and although I enjoy the rush
I keep drowning
and I'm afraid with every push
that I may fall so deep
and only ever see blue
and never reach a coast to breathe again

Perspective

All I wanted was to stay
to have a stronger hold onto what I had left
but you'd refuse even when I begged and you'd say
"I fell apart so often and you only saw the consequences
for yourself"

So silly of me
That in my lowest moment, I expected more from you
When you have never given me your love the way I have always
given it to you

I know what you do
You pretend to care for everyone else to see
But underneath it all, you only care about you

I've created shadows
of my love for you
they linger
like the heavy hold you had
on my soul
but from now on
I'll learn
to leave them behind me
wherever I go

I don't need you
I have the entire world;
I have the clouds
to remind me of better days
and the sun that
provides them for me
and in your absence
I have received both in abundance

And it'll slowly fall away
like specks of dust on your shoulder;
that's how I'll forget you

you can make amends with my heart
but don't use that to your advantage
just because it softens at the thought of you
doesn't mean i have *forgotten everything*

IV: Wind & Wilting

& if your heart must hurt now
imagine how big it must grow
to fathom all of the good things awaiting it
consider the pain as a simple clearing
to happiness
the same way the rain clears the skies
to let the sun in

Sometimes you have to look at yourself in the mirror
As if you're seeing someone else
And tell them to be strong
And that they can overcome anything
Because you and the person looking back at you
Have that capacity within you
That you don't even know until you let yourself
believe it

Just as the rain passed this night
I hope my pain passes the same
and I feel more alive than I had ever been
when I wake up the next day

...because if you keep looking back at your fears, it will become difficult to look forward again where you can overcome them

If it wasn't so hard, you would have never known
you could get through it

Rest your heart
because you're not being fair on yourself
by believing you're capable of coping with
so much more than a person should bear

It's not easy
but I don't want it to be
because then I'll never doubt my ability
to ever make it again

So what is it
that's holding you back
from being happy
for even
a moment
?

I dealt with the noises by pretending they weren't there
When I should have switched them off while I had the chance

Sometimes I'm not sure how I'll get through this
but I keep going on
like a rope attached to my waist is dragging me along
and I'm waiting for the finish line to appear
before my eyes
so I know that after all of it, I managed to survive

Dear God,
i'm ready to leave this torment behind
so tell me
what i must lose of me
to attain peace
I'm ready to let go

It takes a lot of strength
to keep pushing oneself
and still be standing on two feet

Good things don't come instantly
they come *eventually*
You just have to be patient

But look at where you stand
because it took a lot of *climbing*
and a lot of *worrying*
and a lot of *strength*
and a lot of *hope*
to get there

I might be scared right now
but I have to persevere to prove to myself that
if I can conquer this mountain
among all of these hills
I can overcome anything

*You were the most difficult trial I **needed** to grow*

Everything you do now
is for the person
you will be

Every trial is not made
to be overcome successfully
sometimes you need to fail
to learn the same lesson

Don't worry too much, it will be okay
though it may feel like nothing is going in your favour
be patient and strong
and you will find a way

Sometimes I undermine how difficult things get for me
I should appreciate how strong I am for persevering in
situations that are genuinely difficult to persevere in

Recognise all of the things that you have allowed yourself
to become
Be grateful for your own existence

I don't want to be sucked too deep into these worries
oh God,
keep your hold on me secure
please don't let me,
lose me

V: Sunlight & Rain

Black **Rose**   Marah H

You hide me away from the crowd
And let me rest my head on your chest
And I stay there for what feels like 5 seconds
I let out a deep sigh
"I'm sane again"
You smile at the comment, and hold me closer into you

From listening to you talk about something as simple as your day, makes me completely understand how a person can fall in love just like that

I found a bit of you
in everything I wrote
in every thought I held

Maybe it's wrong for me to let them assume that they could
have a place in my heart
when it has always been occupied by you.

You hold a place in my heart
that was built specifically for loving you
and even if you left me alone in this world
I'd still place flowers and light candles
where I can no longer feel your touch
to keep my love alight
that is what you meant to me

Phoenix:

When you call my name for the last time
I hope I burn into ashes to be reborn
so I can spend another lifetime with you

"I love you"
I've said that a million times in my head
but the words never seem to form on my tongue and leave my lips
so I'll let you see it in how I live and breathe for you
and I'll let you feel it whenever you're close to my skin

Compliqué

All I'd need is a canvas
and I'd paint you
chaos

Like anyone else
I could sit here and watch how the sun touches your skin
admiring you in its light
but I want to know you in all the ways no one else can
with the moon uncovering all of the colours you hide

to others, you might be the canvas
but to me, you've always been the painting

<u>& it hasn't turned away since</u>

the day turns into night
and my unyielding heart
still waits
as if, since it has found you
nothing has changed

<u>For you, my everything</u>

And although my heart is hollow
and I have nothing useful to give
I still take these bones apart for you
so you know you have a place in me to live

Black **Rose**   Marah H

Hold me close
warm my cold heart
till I can feel love again

The union of 2

Unravel my layers
open my soul
as if you are searching
for yourself in the midst of me

I will protect all of your wounds
til they become scars
that I'll love
for you are the other half of me

Don't let me go
I'll become so lost in this world without you
that even the moon won't be able to find me

There are so many souls on this earth
yet mine keeps reaching for you

<u>my thoughts keep going but i can't</u>

"if i let my heart go
will you promise that you'll be kind to it?"
it has been stamped on and mocked
but i don't want to hold it back anymore
i want to be free of all restraints
i want to simply *love you*

I'll keep thinking about you until there isn't a part of you I haven't explored in my mind

VI: Blooming

Everything that I think I lack
I've gained in other ways

From every piece I lost of us when you left
I redeemed a piece of me that made me whole again

I don't care if you like me any less
for it has taken a long time for me
to accept the way I am
without feeling the need to change myself
into who you expect me to be.

You are the person you have always needed
So plant your roots in every place that fulfils you
And go about this world like you can't be held back.

Lost in love me land

All of the love I endeavour to find
takes me further from what truly loves me
it's me,
I'm all mine

Who told you that I needed you
to keep me going
when all of this time
I carried enough strength
to find happiness in myself

I just wrote a love poem
and I don't know who it's for
although I thought of us at first
my pen reached the end
and I realised
it wasn't about you anymore

I'm not made to break into pieces
and neither is my heart
I'm made to handle thorns when they prick my fingers
and bullets when they pierce my skin
I'm not made to fall apart

No,
it wasn't easy to love you
in fact, it was painful
but it was never something I'd regret
because I needed you
to know what it felt like to be happy
I needed you to learn that it is possible
for me to be happy by myself

She is the kind of person
that could keep flowers in bloom
during a drought
or a dry monsoon

Like the sky
you remain beautiful
despite the chaos around you

It would take me years to forgive myself
for the hatred I unfairly inflicted
on the soul that
never needed it
and the body that
didn't ask for it

you can't tell your heart
what is good for you -
it decides for itself,
that's why
i've let myself free fall
when it comes to love
and hoped my heart will give me
a *soft landing*

Indestructible

She smiles and stands tall
as if every storm that surrounds her
can't sweep her up in its wrath

I refuse to wager my peace for a temporary happiness
to fulfil my need to receive your love for mere moments
I deserve more than that

I think I had found my soulmate
but it felt like they didn't feel the same for me
and that's how I know
that the most powerful thing I have done
is letting go of the other half of me

There aren't any wounds on my body that I cannot heal
I am the moon with my craters
a flower awaiting bloom

I want a love that weaves effortlessly
into every part of my being
and by love I mean,
with the world,
with myself
and the people that stick by me
I want to fall in love with
just simply existing

I will venture into every little thing my heart desires
I will fulfil every dream that I have
If there is anything that appeals to me even the slightest
I will run towards it without looking back

Starting with me

I can no longer become fixated
on the person I am not
or the person I want to be
I don't know who she truly is
but /what i *do* know is/
she is nothing without **me**

Before you
I never realised how uncomfortable I was in my bones
How I couldn't bear to live in my skin
But you've made me fall in love with it;
Maybe I needed someone to love me as I am
To realise I could do that too

Allow me to first forgive myself
for no one on this earth has tormented me
as much as me

Holding onto you was the worst thing I did
Because it meant that I was letting go of the one thing that mattered,
myself

"occupying' one's thoughts

I realised I started living for you
when I let you take up so much space in my mind
and I didn't leave any room for me to love myself

VII: Growing

We are lucky that such a thing as art exists because if it didn't,
we'd think everything perfect is meant to be beautiful

Even the stars die out sometimes just to be alive again

I should stop hating myself for everything I haven't done
Because I've achieved far more that has helped me persist today
So now,
I should promise myself that I will continue to do more and be more
tomorrow
And the day after
And the day after

After all of this hurt
I realise all I had to learn
was I needed to be broken enough
to never let myself feel like this again

Pretending that everything is okay when it's not isn't going to make you feel any better

Perhaps I was a little harsh on myself
to think that I had the strength to bear a pain so
encompassing
and make butterflies from it

Maybe
if I look around me
I'd see
that I am the cause of my own affliction
because I close my eyes
to the good things around me
too often

It's not the darkness you're afraid of
it's the fear of never seeing the light again

It's time I started thinking
I can make something great
out of what causes me so much distress

I might not be where I want to be
but I'm proud of where I am

I look at myself
and I only see half
of who I could be
that's why I've began searching
in mirrors
for other pieces of me

For once
I'm going to let my love grow beyond me
Without caution
Or fear of repercussions

Leaving you behind

You see
sometimes it's too late when it hits me
I've been waiting for so long for you to see my worth
I've been looking for ways to show it to you
without you knowing how much it hurts
I wanted you to look at me the way you look at other people you
think matter
and I even let myself think about it so often
I can't even begin to put into words
and although I know how sad it is, I still continue to act like you'd
value me more if I put in all of the effort
but I've realised that it's my fault
I let myself live like this first
you weren't the one that put yourself in such a position
I did, and I still let myself worry so much
that I can't find a way to break away from this curse
but I can't blame you
and I can't keep living like your opinion of me can control the way I
live
and I can't keep living like you're the only one who can make me
feel worthy of being loved
or of having the kind of love that I deserve

I am repairing myself everyday
and although the pieces are often too many
I know if I don't hold on
I'll break

Dear God
I trust you with my heart
as I know you won't break it,
but instead you'll make it stronger

*I don't want to settle for anyone less than the person
I have grown myself to be*

Cupid's curse

I will love if I cannot help it
I will no longer deny the aching of cupid's curse
for cupid has taught me to heal faster
than I have ever learnt to hurt

I want to be the person I would have admired when I was younger

You can bloom in so many different colours
don't restrain yourself to the greys and blues
this life may not be beautiful sometimes
but that doesn't mean you don't have to be too

I have never learnt how to pause in life
& that is why
I have never learnt to appreciate
how far I have come
amid the chaos

I've been so afraid of hurting
that I have forgotten to simply live.

Growing begins when you lose fear of the things that lead you to progression

I'm either too little or too much
too full of emotion or empty and numb
yet never enough for you
to be content with me
but I can't change myself
and neither choose to anymore
so accept me as I am
or leave
me
be.

i've let myself be soft
for far too long
& people mistake me
for being timid and weak
but i know that i have grown
in a way that
i will no longer let anyone
walk all over me

i don't believe i was made in this world
to feel like i cannot be free of its cages
i want to live my life in a way that makes me
happy and not feel so *suffocated*

all of these years
and often too
i have felt alone
and misunderstood
and it has made me
so cold that my heart has frozen over

/

but what this darkness has taught me
is that my own existence
is enough to be happy
and find comfort,

i may have a heart full of thorns
but from thorns there are also roses
/and i have fallen in love with both/

I am still in search of a horizon
that would make me feel like my life could start all over again

An acknowledgement

To my muses, my motivators, my mistakes and myself,
Thank you - without you, perhaps I wouldn't have written
this.

/P.S. if you find yourself considering it might be you, it probably is./

© Black **Rose** by Marah H

Original writing, illustrations and photography
Socials handle: @bymarahh/@bymarahh_

Printed in Great Britain
by Amazon